What would the world be, once bereft
Of wet and wildness? Let them be left,
O let them be left, wildness and wet;
Long live the weeds and the wilderness yet.

*From 'Inversnaid', Gerard Manley Hopkins*

# Green Verse

## IN THE MOMENT

### edited by
### Rosie Storey Hilton

Saraband

Published by Saraband
3 Clairmont Gardens
Glasgow, G3 7LW
www.saraband.net

ISBN: 9781916812246

Printed and bound in Great Britain by Clays Ltd,
Elcograf S.p.A.

1 2 3 4 5 6 7 8 9

# Contents

In memory of Geoff Hilton and Jim Storey,
who passed down green thumbs,
wild moors and favourite poems—
all by heart.

# Introduction

Nature, as the twentieth-century writer and academic Raymond Williams said, 'is perhaps the most complex word in the language.' When we introduce another ill-defined word – 'poetry' – to the mix, the complexities, and the possibilities, unfurl even further.

To some, these two words together might bring to mind Wordsworth, in awe among mountains and lakes. It might be Mary Oliver you picture, watching wild geese overhead; Emily Dickinson, identifying hope as a tiny, defiant thing with feathers; or Palestinian poet Marwan Makhoul reminding us that to write about nature at all is a privilege. Others still might shake their heads at all of it, condemning 'nature poetry' as a category in need of serious interrogation, or even outright rejection.

Some see the purpose of nature poetry as being an apolitical celebration of our surroundings; some understand it as a tool for change. This anthology contains a plethora of varied responses to the natural world, but being a collection of 'Poems for our Planet', they combine to showcase the transformative potential of nature poetry as part of the fight for a liveable future, and the struggle for an earth that is not just habitable, but gentler, fairer, and greener.

Nature poetry has been redefined countless times by the centuries and the hands it has passed through, shapeshifting, expanding and unravelling through the various upheavals of our relationship with the natural world, and forever mutating political landscapes. Each person reading the poems in this book will have their own highly individual responses to them, and in this sense, their context doesn't matter; you could skip right on to the poems.

However, our relationship to nature is being politicised by our current, unfathomable shift into climate chaos, and the effects of this can be found woven through the lines of much contemporary nature poetry. This poetry can be powerful not just in helping us make sense of the ecological destruction we are witnessing, but in helping us to resist it. The kind of truth we can access through poetic writing creates an imaginative space in which we can wrestle power from climate-wrecking economies and corporations, and give it back to the natural world. Of course, poems alone cannot save us, but they can change how we think; how we imagine the world might be. And from new ways of thinking comes action.

As well as deepening our understanding of how to protect our planet, there are things that only the natural world can tell us about ourselves and our lives, and that we can only receive when we make time to pause, put our ears to the ground, and our pens to paper. Throughout the process of curating this anthology, the most consistent theme that emerged was that, in our interactions with ecological abundance or loss, we often find our own reflections looking right back at us.

The earliest poem in this collection dates back to sixth-century BC China. Semi-legendary author Lao Zi, or Lao Tzu (now believed to be a collection of people who wrote some of the earliest Taoist sayings, with a single author being invented afterwards) writes:

A sunrise does not last all morning
All things pass
A cloudburst does not last all day

[...]

And if these do not last
Do man's visions last?
Do man's illusions?
Take things as they come.

More than two thousand years ago, Lao Tzu was considering how the cycles of nature align with our personal cycles: ebbs and flows, peaks and troughs, forward movement and quiet reflection. In a contemporary poem also in this anthology, Zain Rishi's 'Gooseflesh', the acts of leaving and return-ing – the ways we come back to ourselves and to the earth – are examined:

> No, your
> body did not forget you. It grew
> with you […]
> Like something that left you, again
> and again, as if that was the only way
> it knew how to return.

These poems are on different sides of almost every seismic event in modern history, yet they share an understanding that there is knowledge to be found in the trees, the seasons and our own bodies; that nothing is permanent, but that everything comes back around, for better or worse. It seems to be a key compulsion of the nature poet, or perhaps just human instinct, to map our messy, changing lives onto the certainty of the seasons.

It is for this reason that this anthology is arranged to take you from spring to winter. Sometimes the season of a poem is named in the text, sometimes it is denoted through specific flowers or creatures, and sometimes it is invoked by an unnamed feeling. Seasons are broad umbrella terms (summer in June is a million miles away from summer in August!)

so within these seasons the poems are organised by theme: winter contains both the retreating feeling of 'dying back' or hibernating, and the quiet sureness that you will soon 'start again', and the days will lengthen once more.

So many of us now are seduced into spending our free time scrolling through 60-second soundbites: lessons on self-optimisation or comedy sketches speaking through twenty layers of irony. I can only imagine – though obviously I'm as guilty as anyone of sinking hours into them – that the long-term effect of this will be to lure us away from sincerity, away from one another, and away from the collective action needed to tackle the climate crisis and other existential injustices we face. Distractions such as these make it easy to forget that we could work together to make our world better, if only we gave our attention to it more fully.

Everyone will have their own thoughts on the seasons that each of these poems relate to, and you may disagree with some – or all – of their placements. But the seasons are something we all share, and in looking at the ways in which our lives and emotional landscapes continue to align with the turning of the Earth, perhaps we can understand a little more about each other. To give intentional time to the reading of nature poetry, to understand where it sits in our lives, is an act of reverence for

the natural world and a way of understanding our-
selves as part of something bigger. At the very least,
it can remind us of what is waiting for us, what gar-
dens might be growing in places untouched by aes-
thetics and microtrends. Nature should invite you
out into the world no matter how messy your house
is, no matter what you have or haven't done, and no
matter who you are. At their most powerful, these
poems will actively plug you back in with that world,
send you out into your nearest green space with
searching hands, prepared to meet the power of the
natural world with your own, and ready to loosen
your grip on your image – in favour of tightening
it around the hands of others and all we have left
to save. The perennial connection between humans
and nature, or perhaps the knowledge that humans
are nature, has never been more worth noticing and
protecting than it is now.

We must also ensure that this movement – both
poetic and political – stays active in keeping its doors
open and its arms wide. Our relationship with nature
itself – with the blackbird, the oak tree or the mud
beneath our boots – is ours alone. But if we love
nature poetry and want it to go on being written,
we must pay attention to who is able to spend pre-
cious time in those wild, green spaces, and who is
not. Nature poetry has the potential to create, pro-
tect and preserve these sacred connections only when

it is accessible to all. When it can include writers of many identities and experiences, each transcribing a universal yet highly specific relationship with the natural world, it has more power; it can transcend more boundaries; it can dissolve imagined borders, interrupt binaries… perhaps even halt pipelines.

In Naomi Klein's landmark book on the climate crisis, *This Changes Everything*, she quotes a rancher in America who said to her, 'We can't save what we don't love, and we can't love what we don't know.'

A poem is a process of understanding and of getting to know, expressed on the page as an utterance of love, or at least of care. If by knowing we can love, and if by loving we can save, then nature poetry is indispensable in the futures of our minds, our communities and our planet.

# Spring

## *Signs of Life*

# But These Things Also

But these things also are Spring's—
On banks by the roadside the grass
Long-dead that is greyer now
Than all the Winter it was;

The shell of a little snail bleached
In the grass; chip of flint, and mite
Of chalk; and the small birds' dung
In splashes of purest white:

All the white things a man mistakes
For earliest violets
Who seeks through Winter's ruins
Something to pay Winter's debts,

While the North blows, and starling flocks
By chattering on and on
Keep their spirits up in the mist,
Spring's here, Winter's not gone.

*Edward Thomas (1878–1917)*

# The Cuckoo and the Egg

Inside the cuckoo's call, the ear of Spring.
Inside the ear of Spring, the swaying reeds.
Inside the swaying reeds, the warbler's nest.
Inside the warbler's nest, the cuckoo's egg.
Inside the cuckoo's egg, the eye of gold.
Inside the eye of gold, the tug of the sun.
Inside the tug of the sun, the bird's wings.
Inside the bird's wings, five thousand miles.
Inside five thousand miles, a vast Sahara.
Inside the vast Sahara, the overwintering.
Inside the overwintering, the hunger for young.
Inside the hunger for young, the earth greening.
Inside the earth greening, the heart's sap.
Inside the heart's sap, the cuckoo calling.

*Linda France*

# At Dawn

*drifting at the Huntington Gardens,*
*San Marino, California*

Alien plant peeps out behind the weathered wood,
botanical surveillance machines loom over the
    sparrow in the hedge:

All eyes out, stalks shiver in the morning air,
    prepare planet descent.
Fog burns off in the cedar air as California
    Towhee sings.

An old-fashioned phone ringer sings across the
    plaza,
"… moved up from the Bay Area," a son says to
    his silver-haired parents.

Oak Titmouse hovers in the lavender, Anna's
    Hummingbird questions
whom she belongs to, why, and what beautiful eye
    shadows

she can make gentle love to, snake tongue, a
    tender whip at night.
Black Doc Martens and a silver vest wrap a
    beautiful humanoid body

# Spring

as fugitive plants crawl toward the mountainous
  borders:
may we escape, you, plant being, me, all us
  travelers in

this Botanical Garden, our dreams of non-
  extractive caresses
a metal line that circles us, holds the ship, sand
  bottom marked by my

Scooter's speeding wheels. Many shoeprints tell of
  older stories.
Black circular sprinklers douse this land, nourish
  growth at night.

Here Octavia Butler walked, deposited her papers,
  and this
wet sweet-sour mandarin taste in my mouth sings
  of Old Earth.

  *Petra Kuppers*

# The Crocuses

They heard the South wind sighing
    A murmur of the rain;
And they knew that Earth was longing
    To see them all again.

While the snow-drops still were sleeping
    Beneath the silent sod;
They felt their new life pulsing
    Within the dark, cold clod.

Not a daffodil nor daisy
    Had dared to raise its head;
Not a fairhaired dandelion
    Peeped timid from its bed;

Though a tremor of the winter
    Did shivering through them run;
Yet they lifted up their foreheads
    To greet the vernal sun.

And the sunbeams gave them welcome,
    As did the morning air—
And scattered o'er their simple robes
    Rich tints of beauty rare.

# Spring

Soon a host of lovely flowers
    From vales and woodland burst;
But in all that fair procession
    The crocuses were first.

First to weave for Earth a chaplet
    To crown her dear old head;
And to beauty the pathway
    Where winter still did tread.

And their loved and white haired mother
    Smiled sweetly 'neath the touch,
When she knew her faithful children
    Were loving her so much.

*Frances Ellen Watkins Harper (1825–1911)*

## Spey Journey

Trunked in deepest jet
are the gean trees; their
blossom a whispering white.

Descending chordal melodies
fall from warbled trees
proclaiming Spring is here.

Tankers of gleaming
steel zip past.
Untitled.

Tormore      Cragganmore
Tamdhu       Cardhu
Carron       Dailuaine

There's the clue.


*Enid Forsyth*

# Spring Song

A blue-bell springs upon the ledge,
A lark sits singing in the hedge;
Sweet perfumes scent the balmy air,
And life is brimming everywhere.
What lark and breeze and bluebird sing,
   Is Spring, Spring, Spring!

No more the air is sharp and cold;
The planter wends across the wold,
And, glad, beneath the shining sky
We wander forth, my love and I.
   And ever in our hearts doth ring
      This song of Spring, Spring!

For life is life and love is love,
   'Twixt maid and man or dove and dove.
   Life may be short, life may be long,
   But love will come, and to its song
   Shall this refrain for ever cling
      Of Spring, Spring, Spring!

*Paul Laurence Dunbar (1872–1906)*

## The Seeker's Guide to Wildflowers

Butter stars in puddled leaves
reach from the wayside:
That's it – *celandine!*
My small hands trace the page,
soft as sea-washed pebbles.

We mark the pages for
*periwinkle* poking its purplish chin,
the modest cheeks of *forget-me-not,*
*bird's-foot trefoil* with puckered lips,
the little hearts of *shepherd's purse—*

we thread arms through brambles,
soil crescents under our nails,
as you teach me quietly:
there is beauty in wildness,
in untamed curiosity.

We preserved those petals,
nectar pressed thin
between soft pages,

but now

# Spring

they float like moths
as I turn to your name,
looped on the inside cover:
*1st form prize, awarded 1953.*

Now I spot clambering yellow suns,
crowding the motorway's edge:
*That's it – ragwort!*
I search it on my phone
but pretend to mark a page.

Can we go seeking again
before the world turns
once more?

*Emma Haworth*

## Into the Woods

I give you permission to puke on my mossy bed.
Honk declarations in orange and green bile,
a collage left draped over my branched bones.

Lose your virginity, backs up against my trunk
skinning your pointy vertebrae in splinters.
Anchor your feet in crusty muddy pats, slip and slide
— It's good if the earth moves.

After, like in films, try a tab, cough up a gob,
leave it dewily glistening on cobwebbed condoms.
Kiddie giggle with gawky giant paws, football
scrawls pen-knifed into my beetled bark.

Too soon, you fly from my nest, but older,
you circle back, to sit in my dank stillness
and rustle in your past – a time before
I opened the playpen latch, and let you go.

*Beda Higgins*

# Cyanotype, by St Paul's Cathedral

when I lay the leaves, bones
and broken bottles on the
chemical paper
you say the sun will bleach it
mark the outline of the trinkets
I've scavenged off the beach

after a while we lift it from the pebbles

on the dark blue scroll
white X-rays begin to emerge

*you see?* you smile
*leave it out in the open air*
*it will tell you its history*

I wonder if I lie on the paper
you'd see the stains from my past too
I squint up into the Southbank sunshine.

will it show my broken heart?

*Tamiko Dooley*

*The Promises You Plant*

## In Jeopardy

Seedpods hang from the wisteria,
a fragile spring surprise.

Tiny shoots of daffodils protrude,
probing bravery in this world

as danger, fire's heat, water's dearth,
are the turmoil that this day surrounds.

A succulent in sand can do no better
than to inch towards a lake.

Will a badger make a choice to tread
with cunning through the undergrowth?

It does what badgers do. It has to eat,
enjoys a habitat that most of us won't know.

But we, reveling in thrill and greed,
deny our behavior's risk, its apathy.

*Linda Conroy*

# O Snail

O snail,
Climb Mount Fuji,
But slowly, slowly!

*Kobayashi Issa (1783–1827)*
*translated by R.H. Blyth (1898–1964)*

## After the Winter

Some day, when trees have shed their leaves
   And against the morning's white
The shivering birds beneath the eaves
   Have sheltered for the night,
We'll turn our faces southward, love,
   Toward the summer isle
Where bamboos spire the shafted grove
   And wide-mouthed orchids smile.

And we will seek the quiet hill
   Where towers the cotton tree,
And leaps the laughing crystal rill,
   And works the droning bee.
And we will build a cottage there
   Beside an open glade,
With black-ribbed blue-bells blowing near,
   And ferns that never fade.

*Claude McKay (1890–1948)*

## To the Miscodeed

Sweet pink of northern wood and glen,
E'er first to greet the eyes of men
In early spring,—a tender flower
Whilst still the wintry wind hath power.
How welcome, in the sunny glade,
Or hazel copse, thy pretty head
Oft peeping out whilst still the snow,
Doth here and there, its presence show
Soon leaf and bud quick opening spread
Thy modest petals—white with red
Like some sweet cherub—love's kind link,
With dress of white, adorned with pink.

*Jane Johnston Schoolcraft (1800–42)*

## To Daffodils

Fair Daffodils, we weep to see
You haste away so soon;
As yet the early-rising sun
Has not attain'd his noon.
Stay, stay,
Until the hasting day
Has run
But to the even-song;
And, having pray'd together, we
Will go with you along.

We have short time to stay, as you,
We have as short a spring;
As quick a growth to meet decay,
As you, or anything.
We die
As your hours do, and dry
Away,
Like to the summer's rain;
Or as the pearls of morning's dew,
Ne'er to be found again.

*Robert Herrick (1591–1674)*

## Promises

Barefoot on the mud                    stalking fruit,
we could get naked, go gardening in gloves
like ghosts playing in the dirt, breathing in friends,
our bodies pinatas to the pierced kisses of the wind
our souls tied to kites paved above clouds
your whispers and secrets pressed in a car park, or
an ancient glass bottle part-sunken into your
                                        neighbour's pond.
the lilypads you surf upon won't be your saviour,
you may grow old with beatings you sow yourself.
but the promises you plant today might grow up
                                        to thank us later.

*Orry Shorys*

## Floating Island

Harmonious Powers with Nature work
On sky, earth, river, lake, and sea:
Sunshine and storm, whirlwind and breeze
All in one duteous task agree.

Once did I see a slip of earth,
By throbbing waves long undermined,
Loosed from its hold; — *how* no one knew
But all might see it float, obedient to the wind.

Might see it, from the mossy shore
Dissevered float upon the Lake,
Float, with its crest of trees adorned
On which the warbling birds their pastime take.

Food, shelter, safety there they find
There berries ripen, flowerets bloom;
There insects live their lives — and die:
A peopled *world* it is; in size a tiny room.

And thus through many seasons' space
This little Island may survive
But Nature, though we mark her not,
Will take away — may cease to give.

# Spring

Perchance when you are wandering forth
Upon some vacant sunny day
Without an object, hope, or fear,
Thither your eyes may turn — the Isle is passed
   away.

Buried beneath the glittering Lake!
Its place no longer to be found,
Yet the lost fragments shall remain,
To fertilize some other ground.

   *Dorothy Wordsworth (1771–1885)*

## A January Dandelion

All Nashville is a-chill! And everywhere,
As wind-swept sands upon the deserts blow,
There is, each moment, sifted through the air,
A powered blast of January snow.
O thoughtless Dandelion! to be misled
By a few warm days to leave thy natural bed,
Was folly growth and blooming over soon.
And yet, thou blasted, yellow-coated gem!
Full many hearts have but a common boon
With thee, now freezing on thy slender stem.
When once the heart-blooms by love's fervid breath
Is left, and chilling snow is sifted in,
It still may beat, but there is blast and death
To all that blooming life that might have been.

*George Marion McClellan (1860–1934)*

# The Deluge and the Tree

When the hurricane swirled and spread its deluge
of dark evil
onto the good green land
'they' gloated. The western skies
reverberated with joyous accounts:
"The Tree has fallen!
The great trunk is smashed! The hurricane leaves
    no life in the Tree!"
Had the Tree really fallen?
Never! Not with our red streams flowing forever,
not while the wine of our thorn limbs
fed the thirsty roots,
Arab roots alive
tunneling deep, deep, into the land!
When the Tree rises up, the branches
shall flourish green and fresh in the sun
the laughter of the Tree shall leaf
beneath the sun
and birds shall return
Undoubtedly, the birds shall return.
The birds shall return.

*Fadwa Tuqan (1917–2003)*
*translated by Naomi Shihab Nye*

## April is on the Way

April is on the way!
I saw the scarlet flash of a blackbird's wing
As he sang in the cold, brown February trees;
And children said that they caught a glimpse of the
    sky on a bird's wing from the far South.
(Dear God, was that a stark figure outstretched in
    the bare branches
Etched brown against the amethyst sky?)

April is on the way!
The ice crashed in the brown mud-pool under my
    tread,
The warning earth clutched my bloody feet with
    great fecund fingers,
I saw a boy rolling a hoop up the road,
His little bare hands were red with cold,
But his brown hair blew backward in the southwest
    wind.
(Dear God! He screamed when he say my awful
    woe-spent eyes.)

April is on the way!
I met a women in the lane;
Her burden was heavy as it is always, but today her
    step was light,
And a smile drenched the tired look away from
    her eyes.

# Spring

(Dear God, she had dreams of vengeance for her
slain mate,
Perhaps, the west wind has blown the mist of hate
from her heart,
The dead man was cruel to her, you know that,
God.)

April is on the way!
My feet spurn the ground now, instead of dragging
on the bitter road.
I laugh in my throat as I see the grass greening
beside the patches of snow
(Dear God, those were wild fears. Can there be
hate when the Southwest wind is blowing?)

April is on the way!
The crisp brown hedges stir with the bustle of bird
wings.
There is business of building, and songs from
brown thrush throats
As the bird-carpenters make homes against
Valentine Day.
(Dear God, could they build me a shelter in the
hedge from the icy winds that will come with
the dark?)

April is on the way!
I sped through the town this morning. The florist
 shops have put yellow flowers in the windows,
Daffodils and tulips and primroses, pale yellow
 flowers
Like the tips of her fingers when she waved me that
 frightened farewell.
And the women in the market have stuck pussy
 willows in long necked bottles on their stands.
(Willow trees are kind, Dear God. They will not
 bear a body on their limbs.)

April is on the way!
The soul within me cried that all the husk of
 indifference to sorrow was but the crust of ice
 with which winter disguises life:
It will melt, and reality will burgeon forth like the
 crocuses in the glen.
(Dear God! Those thoughts were from long ago.
 When we read poetry after the day's toil and got
 religion together at the revival meeting.)

April is on the way!
The infinite miracle of unfolding life in the brown
 February fields.
(Dear God, the hounds are baying!)
Murder and wasted love, lust and weariness, deceit
 and vainglory—what are they

but the spent breath of the runner?
(God, you know he laid hairy red hands on the
   golden loveliness of her little daffodil body)
Hate may destroy me, but from my brown limbs
   will bloom the golden buds with which we once
   spelled love.
(Dear God! How their light eyes glow into black
   pin points of hate!)

April is on the way!
Wars are made in April, and they sing at Easter time
   of the Resurrection.
Therefore I laugh in their faces.
(Dear God, give her strength to join me before her
   golden petals are fouled in the slime!)
April is on the way!

*Alice Dunbar Nelson (1875–1935)*

# Our river which art pure heaven

hallowed be your name
your kingdom lit by the radiant suns
   of kingcups
        your will transmitted by crayfish semaphore
        dart of bullhead, mallard paradiddle

As it is in heaven
the dipper sings
      *give us our mayfly larvae!*
         *Our caddisfly and minnows!*

and we mortals skim stones
notching
      *little*
         *pithy*
            *splashes*

into your silvering skin.

Forgive us our many trespasses
and lead us not into
the temptation
of shareholders or dividends

# Spring

Deliver us from this evil
for yours is the kingdom
your mercurial mountain throats
fluid and fluent
      for ever and ever

            *amen*

*Karen Lloyd*

## Sonnet III

Mindful of you the sodden earth in spring,
   And all the flowers that in the springtime grow,
   And dusty roads, and thistles, and the slow
Rising of the round moon, all throats that sing
The summer through, and each departing wing,
   And all the nests that the bared branches show,
   And all winds that in any weather blow,
And all the storms that the four seasons bring.

You go no more on your exultant feet
   Up paths that only mist and morning knew,
Or watch the wind, or listen to the beat
   Of a bird's wings too high in the air to view,—
But you were something more than young and sweet
   And fair, – and the long year remembers you.

*Edna St. Vincent Millay (1892–1950)*

# A Hymn to the Evening

Soon as the sun forsook the eastern main
The pealing thunder shook the heav'nly plain;
Majestic grandeur! From the zephyr's wing,
Exhales the incense of the blooming spring.
Soft purl the streams, the birds renew their notes,
And through the air their mingled music floats.
Through all the heav'ns what beauteous dies are
    spread!
But the west glories in the deepest red:
So may our breasts with ev'ry virtue glow,
The living temples of our God below!
Fill'd with the praise of him who gives the light,
And draws the sable curtains of the night,
Let placid slumbers sooth each weary mind,
At morn to wake more heav'nly, more refin'd;
So shall the labours of the day begin
More pure, more guarded from the snares of sin.
Night's leaden sceptre seals my drowsy eyes,
Then cease, my song, till fair *Aurora* rise.

*Phillis Wheatley (1753–84)*

# Kingfisher, water, sky
### *for Viv and Nick*

That tell-tale after-flash of cobalt,
the retina's image a split-second
late transferring to the brain

*a dream of blue*
*a certain scattering of light*

it is always ahead
its beak hurled like a hinge-spike
quenched in water

*light undresses, sheds*
*its crimson velvets, its yellow muslins*
*until only blue shot-silk remains*

in slow-motion film
a kingfisher dives,
rises a watery phoenix, scattering
drops like sparks

*from space our blue planet, our blue water*

*and as we go down into deep ocean*
*blue is the last light to go*

   Mary Robinson

# Summer

## *As I was Young and Easy*

# Fern Hill

Now as I was young and easy under the apple boughs
About the lilting house and happy as the grass was green,
  The night above the dingle starry,
    Time let me hail and climb
  Golden in the heydays of his eyes,
And honoured among wagons I was prince of the apple towns
And once below a time I lordly had the trees and leaves
    Trail with daisies and barley
  Down the rivers of the windfall light.

And as I was green and carefree, famous among the barns
About the happy yard and singing as the farm was home,
  In the sun that is young once only
    Time let me play and be
  Golden in the mercy of his means,
And green and golden I was huntsman and herdsman,
    the calves
Sang to my horn, the foxes on the hills barked clear and cold,
    And the sabbath rang slowly
  In the pebbles of the holy streams.

All the sun long it was running, it was lovely, the hay
Fields high as the house, the tunes from the chimneys, it was air
  And playing, lovely and watery
    And fire green as grass.
  And nightly under the simple stars

# Summer

As I rode to sleep the owls were bearing the farm away,
All the moon long I heard, blessed among stables, the nightjars
    Flying with the ricks, and the horses
        Flashing into the dark.

And then to awake, and the farm, like a wanderer white
With the dew, come back, the cock on his shoulder: it was all
    Shining, it was Adam and maiden,
        The sky gathered again
    And the sun grew round that very day.
So it must have been after the birth of the simple light
In the first, spinning place, the spellbound horses walking
    warm
        Out of the whinnying green stable
            On to the fields of praise.

And honoured among foxes and pheasants by the gay house
Under the new-made clouds and happy as the heart was long,
    In the sun born over and over,
        I ran my heedless ways,
    My wishes raced through the house-high hay
And nothing I cared, at my sky blue trades, that time allows
In all his tuneful turning so few and such morning songs
    Before the children green and golden
        Follow him out of grace,

# Green Verse

Nothing I cared, in the lamb white days, that time would
  take me
Up to the swallow-thronged loft by the shadow of my hand,
  In the moon that is always rising,
    Nor that riding to sleep
  I should hear him fly with the high fields
And wake to the farm forever fled from the childless land.
Oh as I was young and easy in the mercy of his means,
    Time held me green and dying
  Though I sang in my chains like the sea.

  *Dylan Thomas (1914–53)*

# A Calendar of Sonnets: June

O month whose promise and fulfilment blend,
And burst in one! it seems the earth can store
In all her roomy house no treasure more;
Of all her wealth no farthing have to spend
On fruit, when once this stintless flowering end
And yet no tiniest flower shall fall before
It hath made ready at its hidden core
Its tithe of seed, which we may count and tend
Till harvest. Joy of blossomed love, for thee
Seems it no fairer thing can yet have birth?
No room is left for deeper ecstasy?
Watch well if seeds grow strong, to scatter free
Germs for thy future summers on the earth.
A joy which is but joy soon comes to dearth.

*Helen Hunt Jackson (1830–85)*

# From 'The Night Wind'

In summer's mellow midnight,
A cloudless moon shone through
Our open parlour window,
And rose-trees wet with dew.

I sat in silent musing;
The soft wind waved my hair;
It told me heaven was glorious,
And sleeping earth was fair.

I needed not its breathing
To bring such thoughts to me;
But still it whispered lowly,
"How dark the woods will be!

"The thick leaves in my murmur
Are rustling like a dream,
And all their myriad voices
Instinct with spirit seem."

I said, "Go, gentle singer,
Thy wooing voice is kind:
But do not think its music
Has power to reach my mind.

"Play with the scented flower,
The young tree's supple bough,
And leave my human feelings
In their own course to flow."

The wanderer would not heed me;
Its kiss grew warmer still.
"O come!" it sighed so sweetly;
"I'll win thee 'gainst thy will.

"Were we not friends from childhood?
Have I not loved thee long?
As long as thou, the solemn night,
Whose silence wakes my song.

"And when thy heart is resting
Beneath the church-aisle stone,
I shall have time for mourning,
And thou for being alone."

*Emily Brontë (1818–48)*

# The Lake Isle of Innisfree

I will arise and go now, and go to Innisfree,
And a small cabin build there, of clay and wattles
made;
Nine bean-rows will I have there, a hive for the
honey-bee,
And live alone in the bee-loud glade.

And I shall have some peace there, for peace
comes dropping slow,
Dropping from the veils of the morning to where
the cricket sings;
There midnight's all a glimmer, and noon a purple
glow,
And evening full of the linnet's wings.

I will arise and go now, for always night and day
I hear lake water lapping with low sounds by the
shore;
While I stand on the roadway, or on the
pavements grey,
I hear it in the deep heart's core.

*W.B. Yeats (1865–1939)*

# The short night

The short night;
Upon the hairy caterpillar,
Beads of dew.

*Yosa Buson (1716–84)*
*translated by R.H. Blyth (1898–1964)*

# Eight Blue Notes

*Chalk Hill Blue*
this down is a standing wave
of coccoliths raised
into the sky unfolding
you are an emissary

*Holly Blue*
on pinnacles proud
of the crumbling churchyard wall
a congregation alights
in spring sunshine

*Small Blue*
mated in the dunes
sheltered from coarse winds
you lay in woolly blossom
a miniature sea urchin

*Large Blue*
caterpillar you sing
the song of the red ants' queen
secreting drops of honeydew
you gorge on their brood

*Silver-Studded Blue*
in the spittle-lined mirk
of the ant chamber
cells reimagine themselves
as shimmering possibilities

*Adonis Blue*
epitome of beauty
captivating your captor
who kills with a pinch
nr Hailsham 9. VI. 1919

*Common Blue*
fallen from Caerulean
a splash of Ultramarine
become everyday
Little Blew Argus

*Long-Tailed Blue*
rare exotic, Brighton-born
uncoil your proboscis
among pea tendrils~
drink deep

*Gillian Dawson*

## The Bluebird

A winged bit of Indian sky
Strayed hither from its home on high.

*Alexander Posey (1873–1908)*

# The Hawthorn Tree

Across the shimmering meadows—
Ah, when he came to me!
In the spring-time,
In the night-time,
In the starlight,
Beneath the hawthorn tree.

Up from the misty marsh-land—
Ah, when he climbed to me!
To my white bower,
To my sweet rest,
To my warm breast,
Beneath the hawthorn tree.

Ask of me what the birds sang,
High in the hawthorn tree;
What the breeze tells,
What the rose smells,
What the stars shine—
Not what he said to me!

*Willa Cather (1873–1947)*

# the bluebells are coming out & so am I

she pulsates her fingers
between the petal folds
of my vulva, the motion is
familiar, takes me back to
summer nights on mossy rocks
the way willow leaves brush
the glossy river's edge,
I am opening in a new way
my thighs stretching outward
like a canyon, she looks up
from my weedy gorge
her face glistening with dew
insatiable, sweetheart,
and mole-like, actually,
beloved to dark crevices
and the warm damp earth
as I climax I picture sparrows hatching
from fracturing shells, bluebells erupting
in an orchestra of purple
mulberries masturbating until fruits
sprout from their wet pink beds
sapphic gulls lovingly raising their egg
It is said when Sappho held a council
with the hetero-Gods
they spiked her with a thorn,
so she licked the iron lovingly

without hesitation, in this way, my love
uses her tongue to hand me a rose
and she is saying, this is yours,
you are mine, *we are glorious*

*Maya Blackwell*

## On Summer

Esteville begins to burn;
   The auburn fields of harvest rise;
The torrid flames again return,
   And thunders roll along the skies.

Perspiring Cancer lifts his head,
   And roars terrific from on high;
Whose voice the timid creatures dread;
   From which they strive with awe to fly.

The night-hawk ventures from his cell,
   And starts his note in evening air;
He feels the heat his bosom swell,
   Which drives away the gloom of fear.

Thou noisy insect, start thy drum;
   Rise lamp-like bugs to light the train;
And bid sweet Philomela come,
   And sound in front the nightly strain.

The bee begins her ceaseless hum,
   And doth with sweet exertions rise;
And with delight she stores her comb,
   And well her rising stock supplies.

# Summer

Let sportive children well beware,
    While sprightly frisking o'er the green;
And carefully avoid the snare,
    Which lurks beneath the smiling scene.

The mistress bird assumes her nest,
    And broods in silence on the tree,
Her note to cease, her wings at rest,
    She patient waits her young to see.

*George Moses Horton (1798–1884)*

# The Trees Don't Know I'm Trans

The trees don't know I'm trans.
In nature nothing genders me.
I stand amongst the trees and exist as another
     visitor in the woods.
A place of neither visibility or invisibility. Just
     existence.

The flowers don't know I'm trans.
For a moment I forget anything but their purples
     and yellows.
They do not stare, question, or stifle.
I sit amongst them and my mind begins to
     breathe.

The earth doesn't know I'm trans
As trans people we are nature,
Discovering beautiful ways to adapt and co-exist
     with itself in journeys of stunning gender
     affirmation.
Growing into our truest selves is a beautiful
     expression of nature, with which we were never
     at war.

*Eddy Quekett*

# In the Garden

I am drunk as clinging bees on the riches of roses,
lung-drugged with apricots and lychee green.
Striped bodies with wings folded
twitching, inhaling sleep
both of us petal-brushed, dew-smeared. We worship,
remembering roses are named after women.
So neglect to time the irises, their ruffled skirts
twirling beyond tomorrow's concerns, and get
   blissed out on breathing:
both madden by scent.
I turn blush-pink, peach-dazed, and kneel before
   shrubs
bee returning to Queen.

*Ennis Rook Bashe*

# A September Night

The full September moon sheds floods of light,
And all the bayou's face is gemmed with stars,
Save where are dropped fantastic shadows down
From sycamores and moss-hung cypress trees.
With slumberous sound the waters half asleep
Creep on and on their way, 'twixt rankish reeds,
Through marsh and lowlands stretching to the Gulf.
Begirt with cotton fields, Anguilla sits
Half bird-like, dreaming on her Summer nest.
Amid her spreading figs and roses, still
In bloom with all their Spring and Summer hues,
Pomegranates hang with dapple cheeks full ripe,
And over all the town a dreamy haze
Drops down. The great plantations, stretching far
Away, are plains of cotton, downy white.
O, glorious is this night of joyous sounds;
Too full for sleep. Aromas wild and sweet,
From muscadine, late blooming jessamine,
And roses, all the heavy air suffuse.
Faint bellows from the alligators come
From swamps afar, where sluggish lagoons give
To them a peaceful home. The katydids
Make ceaseless cries. Ten thousand insects' wings
Stir in the moonlight haze and joyous shouts
Of Negro song and mirth awake hard by
The cabin dance. O, glorious is this night!

# Summer

The Summer sweetness fills my heart with songs,
I can not sing, with loves I can not speak.

*George Marion McClellan (1860–1934)*

*Heat Stroke*

## Joy in the Woods

There is joy in the woods just now,
    The leaves are whispers of song,
And the birds make mirth on the bough
    And music the whole day long,
And God! to dwell in the town
    In these springlike summer days,
On my brow an unfading frown
    And hate in my heart always—

A machine out of gear, aye, tired,
Yet forced to go on—for I'm hired.

Just forced to go on through fear,
    For every day I must eat
And find ugly clothes to wear,
    And bad shoes to hurt my feet
And a shelter for work-drugged sleep!
    A mere drudge! but what can one do?
A man that's a man cannot weep!
    Suicide? A quitter? Oh, no!

But a slave should never grow tired,
Whom the masters have kindly hired.

But oh! for the woods, the flowers
    Of natural, sweet perfume,

# Summer

The heartening, summer showers
    And the smiling shrubs in bloom,
Dust-free, dew-tinted at morn,
    The fresh and life-giving air,
The billowing waves of corn
    And the birds' notes rich and clear:—

For a man-machine toil-tired
May crave beauty too—though he's hired.

*Claude McKay (1890–1948)*

# A summer shower

A summer shower;
The rain beats
On the heads of the carp.

*Masaoka Shiki (1867–1902)*
*translated by R.H. Blyth (1898–1964)*

# From the Bridge

A white brick dappled with grey
Thrown on the river stones or stranded there by high water
Is, on closer view, a gull.
It turns its head dully, blinking now and then,
Unable to know why it is grounded.
Swifts taunt overhead as the sun dies.
At dawn the kingfisher plies the river.
All day the gull is motionless; all night.
On the third morning it is splayed
Wings wide, neck outstretched,
Pressed down by an invisible block.
The shape it makes on the land
Is the shape it would make in the sky,
Could it any longer fly.
It has fallen down the light,
The living eye turning to slate.

*Jill Hopper*

# The Dew and the Bird

There is more glory in a drop of dew,
　　That shineth only for an hour,
Than there is in the pomp of earth's great Kings
　　Within the noonday of their power.

There is more sweetness in a single strain
　　That falleth from a wild bird's throat,
At random in the lonely forest's depths,
　　Than there's in all the songs that bards e'er wrote.

Yet men, for aye, rememb'ring Caesar's name,
　　Forget the glory in the dew,
And, praising Homer's epic, let the lark's
　　Song fall unheeded from the blue.

*Alexander Posey (1873–1908)*

# A Beaching

Ardgay, that great beaching—two tonne whales lifted
in hundreds off the grass to Bloomsbury pits;
truly, it must have wrought a fearful sound, like a planet
dying in the firth that night. Imagine, if
those cleanbone shell holes were found unfounded;
how did a killer whale pod get to Kensington.

And now this, mass casualty on Sunday—
pilots caught out on the bar, crushed within
their own weight on a sealight strand and piled
there like rubber sea defences, cheval
de frise timbers breaking the dune skin of German Bight
after centuries interred. What a traumaed sight.

At the trembling edge, white birds know that something
is up, so get out of the water, wheeling.

*Iain MacLeod*

## polip

Thought that he was real;

Blowfish orange he skittered across the seabed on
claws like *Louboutins*

I didn't know then he was made in Korea, not
malleable exoskeleton like me

For nights I'd curled my tentacles around his neck
as we shared the half coconut as a shelter from
the circling sharks

Even with nine brains I didn't figure him out.
His name *polip* in Hungarian. Mystery always
entices those who live beneath.

We smelt it before the bed waxed and rippled

That iron shaft of holiness through whale bones
and sea glass. A visiting card only Poseidon
possessed. I withdrew as if stung into the
coconut with the synthetic one. His unyielding

plastic bruised my skin,

# Summer

I flashed camouflage colours which ironically
    drew the iron god's flint eye.

Lightning quicksilver fish he launched it,
    dented my fake friend and rendered me
sightless. The relief of unseeing. The iron smell a
    miasma,

I rose with the stone god towards refracted light.

*Emma Conally-Barklem*

## A Dirge

Why were you born when the snow was falling?
You should have come to the cuckoo's calling,
Or when grapes are green in the cluster,
Or, at least, when lithe swallows muster
For their far off flying
From summer dying.

Why did you die when the lambs were cropping?
You should have died at the apples' dropping,
When the grasshopper comes to trouble,
And the wheat-fields are sodden stubble,
And all winds go sighing
For sweet things dying.

*Christina Rossetti (1830–94)*

# What's left Icarus?

Cindering woods with ashen floor
With charcoal fruits and charcoal wood
Smoky flame licking and cursing
The coursing curses of eclipsing concrete lands
Carbon ghost strolling on the naked mountains
Trampling the charred grass and charred corpse
Where a lost river buried her signs
No shelter, no respite from
Ember floor ember sky ember earth
Contemptuous rivers casting a sly look through
    plastics
Tracing the tattoos of animals and birds
Who are migrating into an unknown land
without embracing the gift of life
Ice staggering on a toe in this poem
Speaking a language that translates our future
Time fossilized without forethoughts.

*Pulkita Anand*

# Autumn

## *Losing Our Leaves*

## Sonnet 73: That time of year thou mayst in me behold

That time of year thou mayst in me behold
When yellow leaves, or none, or few, do hang
Upon those boughs which shake against the cold,
Bare ruin'd choirs, where late the sweet birds sang.
In me thou see'st the twilight of such day
As after sunset fadeth in the west,
Which by and by black night doth take away,
Death's second self, that seals up all in rest.
In me thou see'st the glowing of such fire
That on the ashes of his youth doth lie,
As the death-bed whereon it must expire,
Consum'd with that which it was nourish'd by.
This thou perceiv'st, which makes thy love more
  strong,
To love that well which thou must leave ere long.

*William Shakespeare (1564–1616)*

## Curlew Count
### Geltsdale RSPB Nature Reserve

The road curves into surprise
as we come upon the tarn
sitting in the bowl of the land.

Tindale Fell and Cold Fell rise in winter green;
blue is rinsed from the sky
leaving a late November afternoon,
a spill of silver sunlight.

The wetland shines wetness;
light bounces from the re-meandered beck –
nature's game of pickleball.

Had it been summer they'd be here,
dipping their mottled grey-brown
and white feathers in glass-clear water.

*Seventy-three nests with bird pairs* you say,
land haunted by their high-pitched shriek,
wild airspace waiting
for the flute-bird's plaintive tones.

*Shirley Nicholson*

# In Conversation with a Poplar

*New England Forests are Sick,*
   *New York Times October 7, 2020*

You communicate through your roots. Feed your
   brethren,
caution for pests. I believe you speak to me too—
you beckon with breezes, autumn hues, entertain

with shadows and shapes on wretched winter days,
   fill the sky
with vernal bouquets— shade for my sweltering
   summer walks.
Two springs ago a dogwood dropped a branch

on my car—just scratches. Last fall an oak let go
its bough on my husband's car—twisted metal,
broken glass. On a windy, warm October day

I hear a loud crackle just before you plummet.
Grey limbs and trunk strewn across my pebbled path,
dead leaves blown to the road's edge.

If I had not paused by Julie's Barn to marvel
at your kin—maple, beech and birch—
you might have brought me to the ground with you.

# Autumn

Now I walk with trepidation, every rustle and
  creak arouses
like whispered warnings. I'm terrified you reached
your breaking point. Next time I won't walk away
  unscathed.

*Laurie Rosen*

# Home

How brightly glistening in the sun
The woodland ivy plays!
While yonder beeches from their barks
Reflect his silver rays.

That sun surveys a lovely scene
From softly smiling skies;
And wildly through unnumbered trees
The wind of winter sighs:

Now loud, it thunders o'er my head,
And now in distance dies.
But give me back my barren hills
Where colder breezes rise:

Where scarce the scattered, stunted trees
Can yield an answering swell,
But where a wilderness of heath
Returns the sound as well.

For yonder garden, fair and wide,
With groves of evergreen,
Long winding walks, and orders trim,
And velvet lawns between;

# Autumn

Restore to me that little spot,
With grey walls compassed round,
Where knotted grass neglected lies,
And weeds usurp the ground.

Though all around this mansion high
Invites the foot to roam,
And though its halls are fair within—
Oh, give me back my home!

*Anne Brontë (1820–49)*

## no matter what

I draw you closer
for one more squeeze
which you receive willingly,
and then clamber off my knees
to the Lego
and build yourself
a funfair with a rollercoaster
while I wonder what we
have built for you.

on the good days
I draw on you as inspiration
for the re-imagining of the world
we need

on the bad
I wonder how it is I am parenting you
so gently
for a world that will be so hard
by the time you're the same age as me

I know it's just
a luck of geography
that we are sitting somewhere more free
that your school can focus
on maths and spelling
and not bombs or wildfires or flooding

## Autumn

and every day I smell your hair
draw you close and wish you'd stay there
I say I love you
so often
because I can't yet say—
I'm so sorry
that I don't know
if I can keep you safe.

as I teach you
what different colours of food
mean for goodness in your body,
I know that there's a good chance you won't
have those choices ready.

I want to let your beautiful little mind
wander, play and dance
while also grounding it in
collective care and resilience

because the world you inherit
will require that of you as a minimum—
and demand so much more,
that I and those before me should have ensured
would never land on your shoulders
or those other children living now, just by the
    luck of the draw.

# Green Verse

some days I don't know how to look at you
without feeling,
without meaning to—
that have I abandoned you.

but I know it will always bear repeating
for as long as my grieving heart is beating
I will fight for your little life
(and for all little lives)
so no matter what
you'll know I tried.

*Raeeka Yassaie*

## Snow in October

Today I saw a thing of arresting poignant beauty:
A strong young tree, brave in its Autumn finery
Of scarlet and burnt umber and flame yellow,
Bending beneath a weight of early snow,
Which sheathed the north side of its slender trunk,
And spread a heavy white chilly afghan
Over its crested leaves.

Yet they thrust through, defiant, glowing,
Claiming the right to live another fortnight,
Clamoring that Indian Summer had not come,
Crying "Cheat! Cheat!" because Winter had
   stretched
Long chill fingers into brown, streaming hair
Of fleeing October.

The film of snow shrouded the proud redness of
   the tree,
As premature grief grays the strong head
Of a virile, red-haired man.

*Alice Dunbar Nelson (1875–1935)*

# California Redwood in Killarney

I might imagine the immigrant's stance after some
   five-thousand miles
would slacken a bit if still standing at all, what
   could have fallen young
like timber now elder, a cathedral of its own,
   home and far from at once
how deep and wide roots must stretch to wrest
   such deposits out of soil

to feed oneself not knowing hunger, to think slabs
   cut as railway track
connected and carved, land old and new, earth
   riven blossoms of gold
veins exposing a rush of distant figures, of weary
   bones, to find shade
under growth a thousand years, even two, bearing
   other times, places

than the hoof clack of a draught horse drawing its
   carriage over streets,
the jarvey pointing to the tree and the church,
   famine grounds forgotten,
paved now but remembering packed dirt when
   children under blankets
made their way not in laughter as ours but silence,
   and what to do then

# Autumn

with the dead, too many to wake, while the living
   left to say, enough so
we can bury the bodies at least, seedlings never to
   sprout, fallow cones
covered over in shadows of drooping limbs,
   softwood standing longer
than ourselves, and not so much as a name to
   translate the memories

   *Seán Carlson*

## All things pass

All things pass
A sunrise does not last all morning
All things pass
A cloudburst does not last all day
All things pass
Nor a sunset all night
All things pass

What always changes?
Earth . . . sky . . . thunder . . .
mountain . . . water . . .
wind . . . fire . . . lake . . .

These change
And if these do not last

Do man's visions last?
Do man's illusions?

Take things as they come

*Lao Tzu (sixth century BC)*
*translated by Timothy Leary (1920–1996)*

# Smoke

I wake in the dark
and hesitate, tasting the air
like an animal, I am
an animal tasting the air
testing.

It's too dark to see
if the wind has thickened
or light grown dim.
The scent is faint but I know
that's because air
is enormous. It might be coming.

I imagine the weight of it over
the map of the world, the dot of us

beside the shadow that overlays,
overlaps an edge of swelling.
Burning and blood
both taste mineral and sour.

Is it time to close the window?
Is it coming?     It is coming.
Is it yet?               Not yet.

*Kelly Terwilliger*

*Long Live the Weeds!*

## Song of Autumn

Since olden days we feel sad and drear in autumn,
But I say spring cannot compete with autumn.
On a fine day a crane cleaves the clouds and soars high;
It leads the poet's lofty mind to the azure sky.

*Liu Yuxi (772–842)*

# Autumn

In the dreamy silence
Of the afternoon, a
Cloth of gold is woven
Over wood and prairie;
And the jaybird, newly
Fallen from the heaven,
Scatters cordial greetings,
And the air is filled with
Scarlet leaves, that, dropping,
Rise again, as ever,
With a useless sigh for
Rest—and it is Autumn.

*Alexander Posey (1873–1908)*

# Digging

Today I think
Only with scents, —scents dead leaves yield,
And bracken, and wild carrot's seed,
And the square mustard field;

Odours that rise
When the spade wounds the root of tree,
Rose, currant, raspberry, or goutweed,
Rhubarb or celery;

The smoke's smell, too,
Flowing from where a bonfire burns
The dead, the waste, the dangerous,
And all to sweetness turns.

It is enough
To smell, to crumble the dark earth,
While the robin sings over again
Sad songs of Autumn mirth.

*Edward Thomas (1878–1917)*

# Women Carrying Flowers on the Tube

Baby's breath held for the friend who told her
Not to bring anything. Messy kitchen.
Wooden spoon. She's stirring roast red pepper
Soup till it turns from stock to something certain.
Tulips heavy for a bad lover who'll
Comment on the half-ripped price like it's not
Endearing. Who'll sleep soundly tonight while
She draws her maps and makes her plans to run.
Roses for herself. She's got four pop chords
In her headphones and learns this city by
Fantasies. She's in Soho looking bored.
She's got Big Loves. Big Aches cut at the root.
In a corner by a till, only this much is true:
Women, carrying flowers on the tube.

*Rosie Storey Hilton*

# The long night

The long night;
The monkey thinks how
To catch hold of the moon.

*Masaoka Shiki (1867–1902)*
*translated by R.H. Blyth (1898–1964)*

# A flash of lightning

A flash of lightning:
The screech of a night-heron
Flying in the darkness.

*Matso Bashō (1644–94)*
*translated by R.H. Blyth (1898–1964)*

## Wolf, the Word

Wolf. The word is an idea
from an old darkness,
is a pack of shadows
on a moonless night,
is a sword
out of its sheath,
is a guilty conscience
in a wolfless land,
is a prodigal returning
to kill fatted calves,
is a saviour resurrecting
all the hopes of the wild.

*Jim Crumley*

# Inversnaid

This darksome burn, horseback brown,
His rollrock highroad roaring down,
In coop and in comb the fleece of his foam
Flutes and low to the lake falls home.

A windpuff-bonnet of fawn-froth
Turns and twindles over the broth
Of a pool so pitchblack, fell-frowning,
It rounds and rounds Despair to drowning

Degged with dew, dappled with dew,
Are the groins of the braes that the brook treads
    through,
Wiry heathpacks, flitches of fern,
And the beadbonny ash that sits over the burn.

What would the world be, once bereft
Of wet and wildness? Let them be left,
O let them be left, wildness and wet;
Long live the weeds and the wilderness yet.

*Gerard Manley Hopkins (1844–89)*

## Merry Autumn

It's all a farce,—these tales they tell
About the breezes sighing,
And moans astir o'er field and dell,
    Because the year is dying.

Such principles are most absurd,—
    I care not who first taught 'em;
There's nothing known to beast or bird
    To make a solemn autumn.

In solemn times, when grief holds sway
    With countenance distressing,
You'll note the more of black and gray
    Will then be used in dressing.

Now purple tints are all around;
    The sky is blue and mellow;
And e'en the grasses turn the ground
    From modest green to yellow.

The seed burs all with laughter crack
    On featherweed and jimson;
And leaves that should be dressed in black
    Are all decked out in crimson.

# Autumn

A butterfly goes winging by;
    A singing bird comes after;
And Nature, all from earth to sky,
    Is bubbling o'er with laughter.

The ripples wimple on the rills,
    Like sparkling little lasses;
The sunlight runs along the hills,
    And laughs among the grasses.

The earth is just so full of fun
    It really can't contain it;
And streams of mirth so freely run
    The heavens seem to rain it.

Don't talk to me of solemn days
    In autumn's time of splendor,
Because the sun shows fewer rays,
    And these grow slant and slender.

Why, it's the climax of the year,—
    The highest time of living!—
Till naturally its bursting cheer
    Just melts into thanksgiving.

*Paul Laurence Dunbar (1872–1906)*

## October Hills

I look upon the purple hills
    That rise in steps to yonder peaks,
And all my soul their silence thrills
    And to my heart their beauty speaks.

What now to me the jars of life,
    Its petty cares, its harder throes?
The hills are free from toil and strife,
    And clasp me in their deep repose.

They soothe the pain within my breast
    No power but theirs could ever reach,
They emblem that eternal rest
    We cannot compass in our speech.

From far I feel their secret charm—
    From far they shed their healing balm,
And lost to sense of grief or harm
    I plunge within their pulseless calm.

How full of peace and strength they stand,
    Self-poised and conscious of their weight!
We rise with them, that silent band,
    Above the wrecks of Time or Fate;

# Autumn

For, mounting from their depths unseen,
  Their spirit pierces upward, far,
A soaring pyramid serene,
  And lifts us where the angels are.

I would not lose this scene of rest,
  Nor shall its dreamy joy depart;
Upon my soul it is imprest,
  And pictured in my inmost heart.

*Cheesquatalawny (John Rollin Ridge,*
  *Yellowbird) (1827–67)*

## Autumn Leaves

Oh, the gorgeous leaves of autumn!
    Waking long-forgotten dreams
Of the days of early childhood,
    When we gayly gathered them;

Wove them into bright-hued chaplets,
    Placed them on a childish brow,
Dreaming dreams of fame and fortune,
    That we smile to think of now.

Or, with ever fertile fancy,
    Traced we fairy castles fine,
Flowing brooks, and winding rivers.
    In each varied tint and line.

Or we gazed in childish wonder,
    While the trees in beauty shone,
Red and purple, gold and russet.
    Each with beauty all its own.

And the branches gently swaying
    In the soft October breeze.
Gave fresh treasures to our keeping —
    Golden, bright-hued, autumn leaves.

# Autumn

Now we've left those days behind us,
　　And we face the sober life.
All our childish dreams and fancies.
　　Lost beneath its toil and strife.

But whene'er comes bright October,
　　With her wealth of golden trees,
Then again, we're dreaming children,
　　Playing in the autumn leaves.

*Clara Ann Thompson (1869–1949)*

## Navigation

My fitful sleep breaks
In the open air, beneath
A cloud of day moths that paint
Themselves with pheromone trails,
Decoding magnetic fields,
Mapping the ocean's watery maze.

I learned once they drift
Across oceans like this,
Back to their exact point of conception.
A man in a green-fleece-zipped top
Told me that, at a stall,
Where I had only just managed to navigate
A muddy field crisscrossed
With strings and rocks, upright.

Holding a mummified moth
In its plastic coffin, his lightness
Made this tiny, iridescent wonder
Seem like a phantom flicker,
Until the gravity of it hit my body:
*There is so much to know, always.*

# Autumn

That sensation is hitting me
Again, as the haze of moths forms
Itself into a hieroglyph
Above me. Untranslatable,
Shimmering, alive.

*Priya Logan*

## Sympoetics
### *After Donna Haraway*

Trouble in the knots of fertility.
Human fictions, entangled and ongoing,
dying in the muddy compost.
Human beings in interspecies intimacies,
string figures connect seed bags of stories,
overgrown with figures and myths.
I will affirm the fluidity of bodily boundaries,
together with figures physical and nonphysical.
I want to take the mud, fertile slime, animals,
plants, fungi, and form new organisms.
The art of living as a multigender, androgynous
    symbiont;
seductive forms, a persistent unworking of power.

*Frances Cannon*

# Rat and Moon

sleek wet black
of the rat

swimming across the canal
swimming through the moon

splits the uncertain globe
into shivers

*Joan Lennon*

# Winter

## *Dying Back*

# The Garden of Love

I went to the Garden of Love,
And saw what I never had seen:
A Chapel was built in the midst,
Where I used to play on the green.

And the gates of this Chapel were shut,
And 'Thou shalt not' writ over the door;
So I turn'd to the Garden of Love,
That so many sweet flowers bore.

And I saw it was filled with graves,
And tomb-stones where flowers should be:
And Priests in black gowns, were walking their
    rounds,
And binding with briars, my joys & desires.

*William Blake (1757–1827)*

## Museum Tour

I trust the guide — that the dangling carriage
of bones chandeliered above me was once
a whalefall in the depths. I accept the props
of waxed ferns and panther eternally prowling,
always about to launch onto the blue jay. I suspend
disbelief and forget the air conditioning. Dioramas
of a neanderthal drawing horses on the walls of a cave,
and this is supposedly my ancestor recreated (fallow
brows and caressing his smiling child in the loincloth).
These walls are the furthest I'll travel to the savannah,
the taiga, the quarry's housing meteorites. Note the geodes
still radioactive behind glass cases. It traveled
to see me. The pimply guide points at the cocoons
pinned to cork. The violent tender hands that needled
                                        the monarch's wings.

*J.B. Kalf*

# The Voice Of The Willows

Hiding away from the sunlight,
Close by a rippling stream,
Hallowed by childish fancies
And many a waking dream;
There is my royal palace,
Within it my regal throne,
The former, a grave of willows,
The latter, a mossy stone.
And legends of hope did the willows tell
To my childish ears, in that rustic dell.

Here, in my sunny childhood,
I dreamed in my mystic home,
Weaving the fairy garlands
To wear in the years to come.
Friendship, and love, and honour,
They all were to be my own;
The future was strewn with roses,
As I dreamed on my mossy stone.
And still through the leaves, as they fluttered or fell
The breezes sang, in the willow dell.

Visions of hope are departed,
Fairy-like dreams have fled.
The thorns still remain, but the roses,
Like friendship and love, are dead.

# Winter

The breezes sigh through the willows,
I ponder and dream alone
Of the life beyond the river,
As I sit on my mossy stone.
And the breezes sound like a funeral knell,
As they sigh and sob, through the willow dell.

*Thomas Edward Spencer (1845–1911)*

## Poison Your Darlings

you, creature swallowing moss for breakfast
   because you're too
      ashamed to ask for forgiveness
        from your motherland

you, morbid and undeserving
   vile thing who
      repents kneeling while ~~killing~~ kissing
        organs made of ~~carbon monoxide~~ stardust

exalted chalice where I drink
plastic prayers pacified through ink
it's the Sabbath as you beg for mercy for penance
   for peace; yet
      your transgressions tightly embrace spit
       like a departing lover for WWII

what about the young bodies for decors?

I saw your second skin hanging at the antique
   shop last Thursday

oh, sweet mother of ~~God~~ mine
I can't come home (I yearn to be home)
the shepherd looks at me with disgusted unkind eyes
      curse these maggot tears!

*forgive me*
*forgive me*
*forgive me*

I decay back into sacred soil
giggling.

*Agatha Beatrize*

# To Martha, last of the passenger pigeons

You were the last.

Once, you numbered myriads,
Sailing the air, a sea-foam of feathers,
Your wings beating to the roar of my oceans.
Once, rivers ran through your veins,
Your song
A brightness in the day.

Rising in thousands,
You were an orchestra of birds,
Wing-breath rippling the corn below,
Soaring to my steady heartbeat.
A synchronicity of feathers.

And did you catch the solar winds?
Did you skim the hem of space?

And did you know how it would end?
That you would become a memory.
Felled by those
Who have lost sight of home.

# Winter

You rest now in quiet pools of light,
In dark woodland glades untouched by man.
You are the night's benediction, the cloud-nest
That beds the setting sun.
Not lost,
But gone to earth.

*Lynne Phillips*

## The Blue Bell

The blue bell is the sweetest flower
That waves in summer air:
Its blossoms have the mightiest power
To soothe my spirit's care.

There is a spell in purple heath
Too wildly, sadly dear
The violet has a fragrant breath,
But fragrance will not cheer,

The trees are bare, the sun is cold,
And seldom, seldom seen –
The heavens have lost their zone of gold
And earth her robe of green.

And ice upon the glancing stream
Has cast its sombre shade
And distant hills and valleys seem
In frozen mist arrayed –

The blue bell cannot charm me now
The heath has lost its bloom
The violets in the glen below
They yield no sweet perfume.

# Winter

But, though I mourn the sweet Bluebell,
'Tis better far, away
I know how fast my tears would swell
To see it smile today;

And that wood flower that hides so shy
Beneath the mossy stone
Its balmy scent and dewy eye
'Tis not for them I moan.

It is the slight and stately stem
The blossom's silvery blue
The buds hid like a sapphire gem
In sheaths of emerald hue.

'Tis these that breathe upon my heart
A calm and softening spell
That if it makes the tear-drop start
Has power to soothe as well.

For these I weep, so long divided
Through winter's dreary day
In longing weep – but most when guided
On withered banks to stray.

If chilly then the light should fall
Adown the dreary sky
And gild the dank and darkened wall
With transient brilliancy,

# Green Verse

How do I yearn, how do I pine
For the time of flowers to come
And turn me from that fading shine
To mourn the fields of home!

*Emily Brontë (1818–48)*

## Sence You Went Away

Seems lak to me de stars don't shine so bright,
Seems lak to me de sun done loss his light,
Seems lak to me der's nothin' goin' right,
   Sence you went away.

Seems lak to me de sky ain't half so blue,
Seems lak to me dat eve'ything wants you,
Seems lak to me I don't know what to do,
   Sence you went away.

Seems lak to me dat eve'ything is wrong,
Seems lak to me de day's jes twice ez long,
Seems lak to me de bird's forgot his song,
   Sence you went away.

Seems lak to me I jes can't he'p but sigh,
Seems lak to me ma th'oat keeps gittin' dry,
Seems lak to me a tear stays in ma eye,
   Sence you went away.

*James Weldon Johnson (1871–1938)*

## Mire

you should not pause
where salvaged wooden slats sink
beneath the waterline
or on the curve of butterwort

to smell the soggy sphagnum scent
of long-gone picnics
green slime of ham in lunchboxes

                                        sun rotting

you should not pause to see a lizard
dead grey juvenile
or let the burning peat sting

                                        smoky sour

the dunlin says: be here

                                        keep walking

you should not pause to think
about his body

                            as if sleeping

# Winter

nor of sleep

           as if falling
nor of falling

          as if

Helen, you should not pause
where salvaged wooden slats sink
beneath the waterline

there is a watchtower waiting
its wood like skin

> *for S—*
> *as his father found him*

*Helen Sedgwick*

# To Lovers of Earth: Fair Warning

Give over to high things the fervent thought
You waste on Earth; let down the righteous bar
Against a wayward peace too dearly bought
Upon this pale and passion-frozen star
Sweethearts and friends, are they not loyal? Far
More fickle, false, perverse, far more unkind,
Is Earth to those who give her heart and mind.

And you whose lusty youth her snares intrigue,
Who glory in her seas, swear by her clouds,
With Age, man's foe, Earth ever is in league.
Time resurrects her even while he crowds
Your bloom to dust, and lengthens out your shrouds
A day's length or a year's. She will be young
When your last cracked and quivering note is sung.

She will remain the Earth, sufficient still
Though you are gone, and with you that rare loss
That vanishes with your bewildered will;
And there shall flame no red, indignant cross
For you, no quick white scar of wrath emboss
The sky, no blood drip from a wounded moon,
And not a single star chime out of tune.

*Countee Cullen (1903–46)*

# clavicle

In a bed of dried leaves
we noticed the pearly white
of a detached clavicle
lonely like a pulled tooth
ethereal and out of context –
skinless, hairless, lifeless.
We picked it up and carried it away
buried it beneath the tree on the hill
breaking our nails to bleeding
point as we scratched through
the frost-hardened soil.
For the grave we chose the gauntest
tree with bare branches where a bird
had made its nest when the season
provided thicker cover,
abandoned, the misshapen cluster
of twigs and straw hung
like a decaying ornament
or a captured prayer.
There's no difference between
how things seem and how they are.

*Claudia Lundahl*

*Start Again*

## The Darkling Thrush

I leant upon a coppice gate
    When Frost was spectre-grey,
And Winter's dregs made desolate
    The weakening eye of day.
The tangled bine-stems scored the sky
    Like strings of broken lyres,
And all mankind that haunted nigh
    Had sought their household fires.

The land's sharp features seemed to be
    The Century's corpse outleant,
His crypt the cloudy canopy,
    The wind his death-lament.
The ancient pulse of germ and birth
    Was shrunken hard and dry,
And every spirit upon earth
    Seemed fervourless as I.

At once a voice arose among
    The bleak twigs overhead
In a full-hearted evensong
    Of joy illimited;
An aged thrush, frail, gaunt, and small,
    In blast-beruffled plume,
Had chosen thus to fling his soul
    Upon the growing gloom.

# Winter

So little cause for carolings
    Of such ecstatic sound
Was written on terrestrial things
    Afar or nigh around,
That I could think there trembled through
    His happy good-night air
Some blessed Hope, whereof he knew
    And I was unaware.

*Thomas Hardy (1840–1928)*

# "Hope" is the thing with feathers

"Hope" is the thing with feathers—
That perches in the soul—
And sings the tune without the words
And never stops – at all—

And sweetest – in the Gale – is heard
And sore must be the storm—
That could abash the little Bird
That kept so many warm—

I've heard it in the chillest land—
And on the strangest Sea—
Yet – never – in Extremity,
It asked a crumb – of me.

*Emily Dickinson (1830–86)*

## Winter Sketch

On the vanity, under the brass flea market mirror,
beside incense & teapot, menagerie of the signified:
in blue pencil, robin's egg halves loud as cymbals.
Small brown glass vial of nitroglycerine I wafered
beneath your tongue to re-syncopate your pulse.
Bats' raw noses. Paint-flecked aprons of the elms.
Worry stones, river-soft. The sun's smudged thumb
print (it reminds me of you) in a confabulist sky.
Seedpods, red-green & 3D, dehiscent, talismanic.
I have your blue-flame vase of tea roses framed here
in this room, still life on a stained tablecloth, heady
in their white defiance much longer than expected.
Yesterday, in a daydream-remembrance, a holdout:
breach torn in ether, red leaf letting go.

*AJ White*

# Night

The shades of eve are quickly closing in,
    And streaks of silver gild the eastern sky,
Belated songsters have their vespers sung
    With happy hearts and silvery noted tongue,
The busy world has ceased its toil and din,
    And guardian angels now their watch begin.

All nature quiet save the sighing wind,
    And distant murmur of the ocean wave,
Which seem engaged a requiem to sing
    O'er blighted hopes and expectations grave.
The drooping heart its lonely vigil keeps,
    Beside the tomb where proud ambition sleeps.

But memory bids defiance unto sleep,
    And from her quiet chamber, see her creep,
Away she flies o'er hill, and dale, and mead,
    To find the Sacred City of the dead;
Faint not, nor stops to seek a rest,
    Till pillowed on some loved and lost one's breast.

*Josephine Heard (1861–1924)*

# Creatures

The snake plant lives
without blaming ceilings for the lack of stars.

I'll walk a bit before forgiving death for one young
    mind,
count lightened bricks as a comforting thought.

I will get tired,
take a seat next to the greenery.

   *Madina Tuhbatullina*

## My Bonie Bell

The smiling Spring comes in rejoicing,
And surly Winter grimly flies;
Now crystal clear are the falling waters,
And bonie blue are the sunny skies.
Fresh o'er the mountains breaks forth the morning,
The ev'ning gilds the ocean's swell;
All creatures joy in the sun's returning,
And I rejoice in my bonie Bell.

The flowery Spring leads sunny Summer,
The yellow Autumn presses near;
Then in his turn comes gloomy Winter,
Till smiling Spring again appear:
Thus seasons dancing, life advancing,
Old Time and Nature their changes tell;
But never ranging, still unchanging,
I adore my bonie Bell.

*Robert Burns (1759–96)*

# The hazel trees

In the beginning Love satisfies us.
When Love first spoke to me of love—
How I laughed at her in return!
But then she made me like the hazel trees,
Which blossom early in the season of darkness,
And bear fruit slowly.

*Hadewijch of Antwerp (thirteenth century)*

## like a lamb

like a lamb knows her
mother's scent lingering on the lips
of buttercups,
perfume sprayed on the soft hair of grass

as a calf sleeps soundly under a mothers hawks-eye
that in the stillness of a second
becomes doe like, sparkles in the reflection of
her shallow breathing bounty

as a fawn would dip her hooves in the
small islands her explorer mapped out for her
as a cub would prowl, dancing beneath the curtain
   of her protector

like a lamb, i'd find you anywhere
provider teacher shelter
giver taker
and bound, a booming gale, to your side
nestle, be, withdraw,
only to bound back again

our bodies are constellations that i can point out,
on any night sky
they are their own, but they are made of the same
dust fire cosmic liquid soldered welded fixed but
   bending—

they are maps that beget maps,
stones, sticks, running water
the undulating breath of mountains
they are birdsong and sunbeam
like a lamb,
i can find you, in all of this

*Lauren Chadwick*

## The Snow Fairy

### I

Throughout the afternoon I watched them there,
Snow-fairies falling, falling from the sky,
Whirling fantastic in the misty air,
Contending fierce for space supremacy.
And they flew down a mightier force at night,
As though in heaven there was revolt and riot,
And they, frail things had taken panic flight
Down to the calm earth seeking peace and quiet.
I went to bed and rose at early dawn
To see them huddled together in a heap,
Each merged into the other upon the lawn,
Worn out by the sharp struggle, fast asleep.
The sun shone brightly on them half the day,
By night they stealthily had stol'n away.

### II

And suddenly my thoughts then turned to you
Who came to me upon a winter's night,
When snow-sprites round my attic window flew,
Your hair disheveled, eyes aglow with light.
My heart was like the weather when you came,
The wanton winds were blowing loud and long;
But you, with joy and passion all aflame,
You danced and sang a lilting summer song.

# Winter

I made room for you in my little bed,
Took covers from the closet fresh and warm,
A downful pillow for your scented head,
And lay down with you resting in my arm.
You went with Dawn. You left me ere the day,
The lonely actor of a dreamy play.

*Claude McKay (1889–1948)*

## The Oak

Live thy Life,
　　Young and old,
Like yon oak,
Bright in spring,
　　Living gold;

Summer-rich
　　Then; and then
Autumn-changed
Soberer-hued
　　Gold again.

All his leaves
　　Fall'n at length,
Look, he stands,
Trunk and bough
　　Naked strength.

*Alfred, Lord Tennyson (1809–92)*

## Winter Reminiscence

You couldn't wait to trek through
      tundra; see the steps you'd leave behind,
however small. Drained of color, the frozen
      landscape preserved silence
while you built a colony with mittens, your
      wind-chapped cheeks smiling
up at the milk-blue moon. You wished your limbs
      could wear lace as graceful
as trees reaching skyward. If you could paint
      your vision against the desolation,
which would endure? Soon the days will cease
      to pour like maple syrup, refuse
to set like amber stones against snow. When
      the years run swift like sugar
in the runoff, how can you return—to nest your steps
      into those footfalls—if those prints
have all but been erased?

*Cassandra Caverhill*

## Haw Medicine
*Crataegus monogyna*

Because there are days
and, more often, nights
when words aren't enough
and the ones we find
uncurling on mind or lip
fail to take root,
I want to plant you
a hedge of hawthorn.
Named from *kratos*, strength,
it brings the singular gift
of pitching the hardest
wood against the softest
flowers. I offer you this.
Settle back and rest,
watch the black stems
spring into bud, leaf; a film
that captures time, tick,
tick, then releases it.
Let the precious blossom,
clusters of sex and death,
waft their hag-blessed musk
and take you as they will;
a spell to blow the dust
off your winter skin,
what's buried under it,

shy of the lifting light.
May the puzzle of thorn
keep you safe from harm,
remind you of home,
someone, somewhere
whose job it is to take you
in; those open arms,
strong enough to bear
whatever fruit tastes good
to birds, and us,
waxwing and thrush.

*Linda France*

## Gooseflesh

*after Mary Oliver's 'Wild Geese'*

The two-dimensionality of skin
   has always bothered me. The depth
of your bird tattoo being richer
   than mine. How my arm hair only fills
half of the robin's breast. Is it
   a tragedy that nothing about my body
has ever stayed long enough
   for me to miss it? The hole that was put
in my left ear when I was twelve
   sealed itself from the world only to be
opened twelve years later. I let
   the pimples on my back feel the touch
of a lover then break into half-
   moons in the spring.
            And yes, we all become
the ground eventually. It's a kind
   of love, I suppose. The way the trees
lean into the spaces left by felled
   neighbours. The way rain clouds pinch
into the sky like upholstery. No, your
   body did not forget you. It grew with
you like a dog that stopped chasing
   wild geese. Like a fledgling that saw
possibility over the nest, two wings
   racketing against its plump grey body.

Like something that left you, again
    and again, as if that was the only way
it knew how to return.

    *Zain Rishi*

# Emmonsail's Heath in Winter

I love to see the old heath's withered brake
Mingle its crimpled leaves with furze and ling,
While the old heron from the lonely lake
Starts slow and flaps its melancholy wing,
An oddling crow in idle motion swing
On the half-rotten ash-tree's topmost twig,
Beside whose trunk the gypsy makes his bed.
Up flies the bouncing woodcock from the brig
Where a black quagmire quakes beneath the tread;
The fieldfares chatter in the whistling thorn
And for the haw round fields and closen rove,
And coy bumbarrels, twenty in a drove,
Flit down the hedgerows in the frozen plain
And hang on little twigs and start again

*John Clare (1793–1864)*

# Notes and Credits

'In Conversation With a Poplar' by Laurie Rosen was previously posted in *Muddy River Poetry Review*, Spring 2021

'California Redwood in Killarney' by Seán Carlson was first published in *New Irish Writing* in the *Irish Independent* on 25 May 2024.

'The Deluge and the Tree' by Fadwa Tuqan is from *Anthology of Modern Palestinian Literature*, by Salma Khadra Jayyusi. Copyright © 1992. Reprinted with permission of Columbia University Press.

'In the Garden' by Ennis Rook Bashe was first published by Silly Goose Press, in *Issue Two*, on 22 August 2024.